The Power of Storytelling: Unleashing Your Narrative Potential

I. Introduction

Storytelling is a fundamental part of the human experience. Since the beginning of time, we have used stories to communicate, to share knowledge, and to connect with one another. From cave paintings to novels, from oral traditions to films, stories have the power to inspire, to move, and to transform us.

In the 21st century, storytelling has taken on new forms and has become more important than ever. With the rise of social media, podcasts, and other digital platforms, we have more opportunities than ever to tell our stories and to connect with others. But with these new opportunities come new challenges. How do we tell stories that are compelling and authentic? How do we use storytelling to connect with others in meaningful ways? And how do we navigate the changing landscape of storytelling in the digital age?

This book, "The Power of Story: Unleashing Your Narrative Potential," is a guide to harnessing the power of storytelling and unlocking your full narrative potential. Whether you're a writer, a marketer, a teacher, a business leader, or simply someone who wants to connect with others through stories, this book will give you the tools and insights you need to tell better stories and to create more meaningful connections.

The book is organized into five main sections. In the first section, we will explore the fundamentals of storytelling. We'll discuss the basic elements of a story, such as characters, plot, conflict, and resolution, and we'll explore the different types of storytelling, such as first-person, third-person, and omniscient. We'll also discuss the importance of emotion in storytelling, and how to use emotion to connect with your audience.

In the second section, we will delve into the craft of writing and how to create compelling stories. We'll discuss how to find and develop story ideas, how to create memorable characters, how to create vivid settings and worlds, and how to write effective dialogue. We'll also explore the importance of finding your own unique narrative voice, and how to use that voice to create stories that are authentic and compelling.

In the third section, we will focus on the practical applications of storytelling. We'll discuss how to structure an effective presentation, from opening to closing, and how to use storytelling to persuade and sell. We'll also explore how to use storytelling in leadership, how to inspire others and drive change through storytelling. Finally, we'll discuss how to use storytelling for teaching and education, how to make information memorable through storytelling.

In the fourth section, we'll look at the future of storytelling. We'll discuss the impact of artificial intelligence on storytelling, and how technological tools are being used to enhance storytelling. We'll also explore the future of media, and how storytelling is adapting to technological and societal changes.

In the fifth and final section, we'll reflect on the power of storytelling and how it can help us create meaningful connections with others. We'll look at some real-world examples of storytelling in action, and we'll discuss how storytelling can help us bridge the gaps between different cultures and communities.

Throughout the book, you'll find practical exercises and tips for improving your storytelling skills. You'll also find useful resources for writers and storytellers, including books, websites, and other tools that can help you take your storytelling to the next level.

At its core, "The Power of Story: Unleashing Your Narrative Potential" is a celebration of the power of storytelling. It's a reminder that no matter who we are or where we come from, we all have stories to tell. And it's a guide to using those stories to connect with others, to inspire change, and to create a more meaningful and compassionate world.

- **The power of stories: Why they matter for human communication.**

Stories have been a part of human communication for thousands of years. From oral traditions passed down through generations, to novels and movies that captivate audiences today, stories have a unique power to connect people and convey important messages.

At their core, stories are about people and their experiences. They allow us to explore the human condition, to understand different perspectives, and to empathize with others. By tapping into our emotions and imagination, stories have the ability to inspire, motivate, and even transform us.

One of the reasons stories are so powerful is because they provide context and meaning. They allow us to see the world through someone else's eyes, to

—

understand their struggles and triumphs, and to connect with them on a deeper level. In a world where we are often bombarded with information and competing messages, stories cut through the noise and provide a way to engage with others in a more meaningful way.

In addition, stories have a unique ability to engage our emotions and make us feel. They can evoke feelings of joy, sadness, anger, or hope, and help us connect with others on a deeper level. When we hear a story that resonates with us, it can inspire us to take action or change our perspective. This is why stories are often used in marketing and advertising – because they are a powerful way to create an emotional connection with consumers.

Stories also have the ability to inspire empathy and understanding. By sharing stories that highlight different experiences and perspectives, we can break down barriers and promote greater understanding and acceptance. This is especially important in today's polarized world, where it can be easy to demonize those with different beliefs or experiences. By listening to each other's stories, we can begin to see each other as human beings with unique experiences and perspectives.

Finally, stories have the power to inspire change. Throughout history, stories have been used to spark revolutions, to inspire social change, and to promote justice and equality. When we hear stories about people who have overcome adversity or stood up against injustice, it can inspire us to take action and make a difference in our own lives and communities.

In conclusion, stories are a fundamental part of human communication. They allow us to connect with each other, to understand different perspectives, and to engage our emotions and imagination. Whether it's a personal anecdote shared with friends, a novel that transports us to a different world, or a movie that inspires us to take action, stories have a unique power to shape our lives and the world around us.

- **Storytelling in the digital age: How storytelling has changed in the 21st century**

The digital age has brought about significant changes in the way we tell stories. With the advent of social media, blogs, and other online platforms, storytelling has become more accessible and diverse than ever before. Here are some ways in which storytelling has changed in the 21st century:

1. New mediums: The rise of digital platforms has opened up new mediums for storytelling. From short-form videos on TikTok to long-form articles on Medium, there are now countless ways to tell stories online. Additionally, virtual and augmented reality technologies are creating new possibilities for immersive storytelling.

2. Global reach: The internet has made it possible to reach audiences all around the world. Stories that may have been confined to a local audience in the past can now be shared with a global audience through social media, blogs, and other online platforms.

3. User-generated content: Social media platforms like Instagram and YouTube have given rise to user-generated content, allowing anyone to become a storyteller. This has led to a democratization of storytelling, giving voices to those who may have been marginalized in traditional media.

4. Interactive storytelling: Digital platforms have also made it possible to create interactive stories, where readers or viewers can participate in the story and affect its outcome. This can create a more engaging and immersive experience for the audience.

5. Data-driven storytelling: The digital age has also made it possible to use data to inform and enhance storytelling. With access to data analytics, storytellers can better understand their audience and create content that resonates with them.

However, these changes also bring new challenges. With so much content available online, it can be difficult to capture and hold an audience's attention. Additionally, the ease of creating and sharing content means that there is a lot of noise to cut through to get your message heard.

In conclusion, storytelling in the digital age has brought about significant changes in the way we tell stories. While these changes have opened up new possibilities and opportunities, they also present new challenges. To be successful in the 21st century, storytellers must adapt to these changes and find ways to stand out in an increasingly crowded online landscape.

II. Storytelling Fundamentals

- **The basic elements of a story: Characters, plot, conflict, and resolution**

At the heart of every great story are four basic elements: characters, plot, conflict, and resolution. These elements are the building blocks of narrative and are essential for creating a compelling story that engages and resonates with readers.

Characters are the people or entities who populate a story. They are the ones who drive the action forward and bring the story to life. Without characters, there is no story. When crafting characters, it's important to create fully realized individuals with their own unique personalities, motivations, and flaws. The more complex and multi-dimensional the characters are, the more engaging and relatable the story will be.

The plot is the sequence of events that unfolds in a story. It's what happens to the characters and how they react to those events. A good plot is one that is well-crafted and engaging, with twists and turns that keep readers on the edge of their seats. The best plots are ones that have a clear arc, with a beginning, middle, and end that are tied together by a central theme or idea.

Conflict is what drives the plot forward and creates tension in the story. It's the clash between the characters and their desires, or the external forces that they must overcome. Conflict can take many forms, including internal conflicts within a character's own psyche or external conflicts between characters or groups of characters. The key is to create a conflict that is compelling and meaningful, one that forces the characters to grow and change over the course of the story.

Resolution is the point at which the conflict is resolved and the story comes to a close. It's the moment of catharsis for the reader, where they feel a sense of closure and satisfaction with the story's conclusion. The best resolutions are ones that tie up all the loose ends and leave the reader with a sense of understanding and fulfillment.

But while these elements may seem straightforward, there is an art to crafting them in a way that truly resonates with readers. Here are some tips for incorporating these elements into your own storytelling:

1. Create fully realized characters: Your characters should be multi-dimensional, with their own unique personalities, motivations, and flaws. Give them backgrounds and backstories that help the reader understand who they are and what drives them.

2. Develop a compelling plot: Your plot should be well-crafted and engaging, with twists and turns that keep readers guessing. Make sure that there is a clear arc to the story, with a beginning, middle, and end that are tied together by a central theme or idea.

3. Build tension through conflict: Conflict is what creates tension in the story and drives the plot forward. Make sure that the conflict is meaningful and compelling, and that it forces the characters to grow and change over the course of the story.

4. Create a satisfying resolution: Your resolution should tie up all the loose ends and leave the reader with a sense of understanding and fulfillment. Make sure that the resolution is consistent with the rest of the story and that it provides a sense of closure for the reader.

Ultimately, the basic elements of a story are what make it memorable and powerful. By crafting fully realized characters, developing a compelling plot, building tension through conflict, and creating a satisfying resolution, you can create a story that engages and resonates with readers. Whether you're writing a novel, a short story, or a screenplay, these elements are essential for unleashing your narrative potential and creating stories that will stand the test of time.

Creating an effective narrative structure is essential to crafting a story that engages and resonates with readers. One of the most commonly used models for structuring a story is the dramatic arc, which follows a basic pattern of exposition, rising action, climax, falling action, and resolution.

Exposition is the beginning of the story, where the reader is introduced to the characters and the setting. It's where the groundwork is laid for the story to come, and where the reader begins to get a sense of what the story is about. The key to effective exposition is to provide enough detail to set the stage without overwhelming the reader with too much information.

Rising action is the part of the story where the tension begins to build. It's where the characters face challenges and obstacles that they must overcome. This is where the conflict of the story is introduced, and where the stakes are raised for the characters. The key to effective rising action is to keep the tension building, with each new challenge more difficult and more significant than the last.

Climax is the high point of the story, where the conflict comes to a head and the fate of the characters hangs in the balance. This is where the most intense action of the story takes place, and where the reader is on the edge of their seat, wondering what will happen next. The key to effective climax is to make it as intense and gripping as possible, with high stakes and a sense of danger for the characters.

Falling action is the part of the story where the tension begins to ease. It's where the characters begin to resolve the conflict and tie up loose ends. This is where the reader begins to get a sense of how the story will end, and where they start to feel a sense of closure.

Resolution is the end of the story, where all the loose ends are tied up and the reader gets a sense of how the characters have been affected by the events of the story. The key to effective resolution is to make it satisfying for the reader, with a sense of closure and a feeling that the story has been resolved in a meaningful way.

While the dramatic arc is a popular model for structuring a story, it's not the only one. There are many other models that can be used, depending on the type of story you're telling and the effect you want to create. Some other models include:

- The hero's journey: This model follows the journey of a hero as they overcome challenges and obstacles to achieve a goal. It's often used in adventure and fantasy stories, and is characterized by a series of stages that the hero must pass through, such as the call to adventure, the threshold, the challenges and tests, and the ultimate goal.

- Three-act structure: This model divides the story into three parts: setup, confrontation, and resolution. The setup introduces the characters and the setting, the confrontation is where the conflict is introduced and the tension begins to build, and the resolution is where the conflict is resolved and the story comes to a close.

- The five-act structure: This model divides the story into five parts: exposition, rising action, climax, falling action, and denouement. The denouement is similar to the resolution in the dramatic arc model, but it focuses more on the aftermath of the story and the long-term effects on the characters.

No matter which models you choose to use, the key to effective narrative structure is to create a story that engages and resonates with readers. This means creating well-developed characters, a compelling plot, and a conflict that is meaningful and compelling. By using a model like the dramatic arc, the hero's journey, or the three-act structure, you can create a structure that supports your story and helps you to achieve your storytelling goals.

There are various types of storytelling styles that an author can use to tell a story. Each type of storytelling offers unique advantages and disadvantages, depending on the kind of story an author wants to tell. Here are some of the most common types of storytelling styles:

1. First-person: This type of storytelling involves telling the story from the perspective of one of the characters in the story. First-person storytelling creates an intimate and personal connection between the reader and the protagonist. It can be useful for creating a strong voice and immersing the reader in the character's thoughts and feelings. However, it can also limit the scope of the story, as the reader only has access to the protagonist's perspective.

2. Third person limited: This type of storytelling involves telling the story from an external perspective, but limiting the narration to the thoughts and feelings of one character. Third-person limited storytelling allows the author to provide a broader perspective than first-person, while still maintaining a close connection to the

protagonist. However, it can still limit the reader's access to other characters' thoughts and feelings.

3. Third-person omniscient: This type of storytelling involves telling the story from an external perspective that is not limited to any one character. Third-person omniscient allows the author to provide a more comprehensive view of the story and its characters. This can be useful for epic stories with multiple characters and complex plotlines. However, it can also be difficult to maintain a strong connection between the reader and the characters, as the reader may feel more removed from their thoughts and feelings.

4. Second-person: This type of storytelling involves addressing the reader directly as if they were a character in the story. Second-person storytelling is less common than other types, but it can be useful for creating an immersive experience and making the reader feel like they are part of the story. However, it can also be difficult to maintain this perspective over the course of a longer narrative.

5. Epistolary: This type of storytelling involves telling the story through letters, diary entries, or other forms of written communication between characters. Epistolary storytelling can create a sense of immediacy and authenticity, as the reader is able to read the characters' own words. It can also be useful for creating suspense, as the reader may not know what has happened to the characters since the last letter or entry. However,

it can be challenging to maintain this format for the entire length of a story.

6. Nonlinear: This type of storytelling involves telling the story out of chronological order. Nonlinear storytelling can be useful for creating suspense, exploring themes of memory and perception, and adding complexity to the plot. However, it can also be challenging to keep the reader engaged and to avoid confusion.

Each of these types of storytelling has its own strengths and weaknesses, and an author should choose the style that best suits the story they want to tell. Experimenting with different types of storytelling can also help authors find their own unique voice and style. By understanding the different types of storytelling, authors can better unleash their narrative potential and create stories that engage and resonate with readers.

- **The role of emotion in storytelling: How to make people connect with your story**

Emotion is a fundamental aspect of storytelling. Stories that resonate with readers are often those that evoke strong emotions, whether it be joy, sadness, anger, or fear. Emotions help readers connect with characters and the events of the story, creating a deeper sense of immersion and engagement.

So, how can an author effectively use emotion in their storytelling? Here are some tips to consider:

1. Know your audience: Different readers will have different emotional triggers. What makes one reader feel deeply moved might not have the same effect on another. Understanding your target audience is essential for identifying the emotions that will resonate with them.

2. Create relatable characters: Readers are more likely to connect emotionally with characters they can relate to. Developing complex and multifaceted characters that have flaws and strengths can help readers see themselves in the characters and become invested in their stories.

3. Show, don't tell: It's often said that good writing shows, rather than tells, the story. This is especially true when it comes to emotions. Instead of simply stating that a character is sad or happy, use descriptive language and sensory details to show how the character feels.

4. Use dialogue effectively: Dialogue can be a powerful tool for conveying emotion. Consider how characters speak to each other and the emotions that are expressed through their words. Use body language and facial expressions to further enhance the emotional impact of the dialogue.

5. Create tension: Conflict is at the heart of any good story. By creating tension between characters or within the plot, authors can evoke a range of emotions in their readers. Whether it be a romantic tension, a rivalry, or a life-or-death

situation, tension can keep readers engaged and invested in the story.

6. Use pacing to build emotion: The pacing of a story can also impact how readers connect emotionally with the narrative. By varying the pace, authors can create moments of tension, excitement, or introspection, evoking different emotions in their readers.

7. Appeal to the senses: Sensory details can help readers connect with a story on a deeper level. By describing the sights, sounds, smells, tastes, and textures of a scene, authors can create a more immersive experience for their readers, increasing the emotional impact of the story.

8. Use symbolism and metaphor: Symbolism and metaphor can be powerful tools for conveying emotions indirectly. For example, a character's physical appearance or surroundings can be used to convey their emotional state without directly stating it.

9. Be authentic: Authenticity is crucial when it comes to emotional storytelling. Readers can often sense when emotions feel forced or contrived. By drawing on personal experiences and emotions, authors can create stories that feel genuine and authentic, allowing readers to connect on a deeper level.

10. End with a satisfying emotional payoff: The emotional payoff of a story is often what sticks with readers long after they've finished reading.

By creating a satisfying emotional resolution, authors can leave readers feeling fulfilled and satisfied, deepening their connection with the story.

Ultimately, the key to effective emotional storytelling is to create a narrative that connects with readers on a personal level. By using relatable characters, descriptive language, tension, and pacing, authors can create stories that evoke a range of emotions and leave a lasting impact on their readers. Emotion is a powerful tool for any storyteller, and by tapping into this fundamental aspect of human experience, authors can unleash their narrative potential and create stories that resonate with readers long after they've finished reading.

III. Crafting Stories

- **How to find and develop story ideas**

As a storyteller, one of the biggest challenges is finding and developing compelling story ideas. Whether you're a novelist, a screenwriter, or a marketer, your success ultimately hinges on your ability to captivate your audience with your stories. In this chapter, we'll explore some techniques for generating and developing story ideas that will engage your audience and help you stand out in a crowded market.
Look to Your Life

1. One of the most accessible sources of story ideas is your own life experiences. Your personal story is unique to you, and there are countless ways to draw inspiration from it. Consider the challenges you've faced, the lessons you've learned, and the people you've met along the way. Think about the moments that have made you laugh, cry, or feel deeply. These can all be rich sources of material for your storytelling.

    Explore Other People's Stories

2. Another great way to find story ideas is to look to the stories of others. Read books, watch movies, and listen to podcasts that interest you. Look for stories that move you, that make you think, or that challenge your perspective. Take note of the characters, the conflicts, and the themes that resonate with you. Analyze what makes these stories effective and

---

consider how you might apply those principles to your own work.

Play the "What If?" Game

3.   One of the most useful techniques for generating story ideas is to play the "What if?" game. This involves taking a familiar situation and asking yourself what might happen if one key element were changed. For example, what if a young woman discovered she had the ability to time travel? What if a detective investigating a murder was actually the killer? The possibilities are endless, and this technique can be a powerful tool for unlocking your creativity.

Use Prompts and Exercises

4.   If you're struggling to come up with story ideas, there are a variety of writing prompts and exercises available that can help jumpstart your creativity. These might include prompts like "write a story from the perspective of a tree" or exercises like "describe a room in vivid detail." By forcing yourself to approach storytelling from a different angle, you may be able to discover new ideas and perspectives that you wouldn't have thought of otherwise.

Collaborate with Others

5.   Sometimes the best way to find story ideas is to collaborate with others. Join a writing group or a workshop and work with other storytellers to develop your ideas. Brainstorm together, provide feedback on

each other's work, and collaborate on projects. Two heads are often better than one, and by working with others, you may be able to develop ideas that you wouldn't have thought of on your own.

Once you've generated some story ideas, the next step is to develop them into fully fleshed-out stories. This process can involve outlining, character development, research, and more. The key is to keep an open mind and be willing to explore different avenues until you find the story that resonates with you and your audience. With practice and persistence, you can become a master storyteller capable of captivating your audience with the power of your words.

- **How to create memorable characters: Traits, motivations, and conflicts**

When it comes to creating a compelling story, one of the most important elements is the characters. A good character can make or break a story, and can leave a lasting impression on the reader or viewer. In this chapter, we'll discuss how to create memorable characters by exploring their traits, motivations, and conflicts.

Traits

One of the first things to consider when creating a character is their traits. This includes their physical appearance, personality, values, and beliefs. These traits should be consistent throughout the story, as they help to create a sense of continuity and help the reader or viewer to connect with the character.

When it comes to physical appearance, you don't have to go into too much detail, but you should give enough information for the reader or viewer to picture the character in their mind. For personality traits, think about what makes the character unique. Are they outgoing or introverted? Optimistic or pessimistic? Brave or cowardly? These traits will help to shape the character's behavior and reactions throughout the story.

Values and beliefs are also important to consider, as they will impact the character's decisions and actions. For example, if a character values loyalty above all else, they may go to great lengths to protect their friends and family. On the other hand, if a character believes that the ends justify the means, they may be willing to do whatever it takes to achieve their goals.

Motivations

Another key element in creating a memorable character is understanding their motivations. What drives the character to take action? What are their goals, and what are they willing to sacrifice to achieve them?

One effective way to explore a character's motivations is to use the "why" technique. For example, if a character decides to risk their life to save someone else, ask yourself why they made that decision. Perhaps they have a strong sense of duty or feel a deep connection to the person they are saving. By understanding the character's motivations, you can create a more believable and relatable character.

Conflicts

Finally, conflicts are essential to creating memorable characters. These conflicts can come in many forms, from external conflicts such as battles or natural disasters, to internal conflicts such as self-doubt or conflicting emotions.

One effective way to create conflicts is to use the character's traits and motivations against them. For example, if a character is fiercely independent, they may struggle to ask for help when they need it. If a character values honesty above all else, they may struggle to keep a secret that could hurt someone they care about. By creating conflicts that challenge the character's beliefs and values, you can create a more engaging and dynamic story.

Conclusion

Creating memorable characters is essential to creating a compelling story. By carefully considering a character's traits, motivations, and conflicts, you can create characters that are relatable, interesting, and unforgettable. Whether you're writing a novel, a screenplay, or any other type of story, taking the time to develop your characters will pay off in the long run.

- **How to create vivid settings and worlds: The importance of description and setting**

The setting of a story is not just a backdrop, but an integral part of the narrative that can evoke powerful emotions and create a rich atmosphere for the reader.

A well-crafted setting can transport the reader to another time, place, or even world, making the story more engaging and immersive. In this chapter, we will explore the importance of setting in storytelling and how to create vivid settings and worlds that will leave a lasting impression on your audience.

Importance of Setting

The setting is the physical and cultural environment in which the story takes place. It includes the time, place, and social context in which the characters exist. Setting can be a powerful tool for establishing mood and tone, and can even be used as a metaphor for the story's theme. A bleak and desolate landscape can create a sense of isolation and hopelessness, while a vibrant and colorful world can convey a sense of joy and excitement.

Setting can also help to establish the rules of the story's universe. In a fantasy or science fiction story, for example, the setting may include magical or futuristic elements that are unique to that world. This helps to create a sense of verisimilitude and allows the reader to suspend disbelief and become fully immersed in the story.

Creating Vivid Settings

To create a vivid setting, you must use descriptive language that engages the reader's senses. This includes not only visual details, but also sounds, smells, and textures. By evoking the reader's senses, you can create a more immersive experience that will keep them engaged in the story.

One effective technique for creating a vivid setting is to use specific details that are unique to the environment. For example, if your story takes place in a forest, you might describe the way the sunlight filters through the leaves, the sound of birds chirping, or the smell of pine needles. These specific details can help to create a sense of place that is unique to your story.

Another technique for creating a vivid setting is to use metaphors and similes. By comparing the setting to something else, you can create a more vivid image in the reader's mind. For example, you might describe a city skyline as a row of jagged teeth, or a river as a serpent winding through the landscape.

The Importance of Research

If you are writing a story set in a real-world location or time period, it is important to do your research to ensure that your setting is accurate and authentic. This can involve reading historical accounts, visiting the location, or talking to experts in the field. By doing your research, you can create a setting that feels real and authentic, which can help to immerse the reader in the story.

Creating Imaginary Worlds

In fantasy or science fiction stories, the setting may be an entirely imaginary world that exists only in the author's imagination. In these cases, the author must create a world that is internally consistent and believable. This can involve creating a history, culture, and geography for the world, as well as establishing the rules that govern its magic or technology.

One effective technique for creating an imaginary world is to start with a small detail and build out from there. For example, you might start with a single city and then develop the surrounding landscape, culture, and history. This can help to create a more organic and believable world that feels like it could exist.

Another technique for creating an imaginary world is to draw inspiration from the real world. By taking elements from different cultures, time periods, or geographic locations, you can create a world that feels unique and interesting. This can help to make your world more engaging and immersive for the reader.

- **How to write effective dialogue: The art of conversation in fiction and nonfiction**

Dialogue is a fundamental aspect of storytelling that can help bring characters to life and move the plot forward. Whether you are writing fiction or nonfiction, mastering the art of conversation is essential to creating engaging and memorable stories.
Effective dialogue should feel natural and realistic, while also serving a purpose in advancing the story or developing characters. Here are some tips for writing compelling dialogue:

1. Make it sound authentic: One of the most important things about writing dialogue is making it sound like real conversation. Listen to the way people talk in everyday life, paying attention to their word choices, sentence structure, and the rhythm of their speech. Avoid

overly formal or stilted language, and strive for a natural and conversational tone.

2. Use dialogue to reveal character: Dialogue can be a powerful tool for revealing character traits and motivations. Consider the way each character speaks and the language they use, as well as their tone, inflection, and body language. What do these details say about the character's personality, background, or emotional state?

3. Keep it concise: In real life, people often ramble or go off on tangents during conversation, but in fiction and nonfiction, dialogue should be concise and purposeful. Avoid unnecessary small talk or filler dialogue, and focus on moving the story forward or revealing important information.

4. Use subtext: Sometimes what characters don't say is just as important as what they do say. Using subtext, or the underlying meaning or implications behind dialogue, can add depth and complexity to your characters and their interactions.

5. Vary sentence length and structure: Varying the length and structure of sentences in dialogue can help create a more natural and engaging rhythm. Short, snappy sentences can convey urgency or tension, while longer, more complex sentences can reflect a character's thought process or emotional state.

6. Avoid exposition: Dialogue should be used to reveal information and move the story forward,

but be careful not to rely too heavily on exposition. Instead, try to weave important details into the conversation in a way that feels natural and organic.

7. Read it aloud: Once you have written a scene of dialogue, read it aloud to see how it sounds. Does it flow naturally? Is the pacing consistent? Are there any awkward or clunky sentences that need to be revised?

In addition to these tips, there are also different approaches to writing dialogue that can be effective depending on the type of story you are telling. Here are some examples:

1. Realistic dialogue: This approach aims to capture the way people actually talk in real life, using natural language and incorporating pauses, interruptions, and other elements of natural conversation. This style can be effective for creating a sense of realism and authenticity, but it can also be challenging to write and may not always serve the story.

2. Elevated dialogue: Elevated dialogue uses more formal language and syntax, often incorporating elements of poetry or rhetoric. This style can be effective for creating a sense of grandeur or heightened emotion, but it can also come across as artificial or melodramatic if not executed well.

3. Minimalist dialogue: Minimalist dialogue is characterized by short, sparse sentences that convey a lot with very few words. This style can

be effective for creating tension or emphasizing certain emotions, but it can also feel too sparse or cryptic if overused.

4. Vernacular dialogue: Vernacular dialogue incorporates regional dialects or colloquialisms, aiming to capture the unique flavor of a particular place or culture. This style can be effective for creating a sense of authenticity and place, but it can also be difficult to read if the dialect is too heavy or confusing.

In conclusion, dialogue is a powerful tool for creating compelling stories that engage and entertain readers. Whether you are writing fiction or nonfiction, mastering the art of conversation can help you to create amazing stories.

- **The importance of narrative voice: How to find your unique style and voice**

Narrative voice is the personality and style of a writer that comes through in their writing. It is what sets one writer apart from another, and can make a story feel unique and memorable. Finding your own voice can be a challenge, but it is an essential part of becoming a successful writer. In this chapter, we will explore the importance of narrative voice and how to find your own unique style.

Why is narrative voice important?

Narrative voice is important because it can make or break a story. A strong, unique voice can draw readers in and keep them engaged, while a weak or generic voice can leave readers feeling disconnected and uninterested. A strong voice can also help you stand out in a crowded marketplace, making it easier for readers to remember your work and return for more.

Additionally, narrative voice can shape the tone and mood of a story. It can convey emotions and create atmosphere, setting the stage for the events of the story to unfold. The way you choose to tell your story can make a big difference in how readers perceive it, and narrative voice is a key element in creating that perception.

How to find your narrative voice

Finding your narrative voice can be a challenge, but it is a process that every writer must go through. Here are some tips to help you find your own unique style and voice:

1. Read widely and critically: Reading is one of the best ways to develop your writing skills and find your own voice. Read books in your genre, as well as those outside of it. Pay attention to how other writers use language and structure their stories. Consider what works and what doesn't, and apply those lessons to your own writing.

2. Write every day: Writing every day is essential for developing your writing skills and finding your voice. Make time to write, even if it's just for a few minutes each day. The more you write, the more comfortable you will become with your own style and voice.

3. Experiment with different styles: Don't be afraid to try new things and experiment with different styles. Write in different genres and styles to see what works best for you. This can help you find your own unique voice and style.

4. Focus on your strengths: Everyone has their own strengths and weaknesses as a writer. Focus on your strengths and build on them. This can help you develop a unique voice that sets you apart from other writers.

5. Be true to yourself: Ultimately, the key to finding your narrative voice is to be true to yourself. Write from the heart and let your own personality and style shine through. Don't try to imitate other writers or write in a style that doesn't feel natural to you.

Tips for developing your narrative voice.

Once you've found your narrative voice, it's important to continue developing and refining it. Here are some tips for doing so:

1. Write with intention: Every word and sentence in your story should serve a purpose. Write with intention and make sure that every aspect of your story, from the characters to the setting, contributes to the overall narrative.

2. Use vivid language: Your choice of language can help bring your story to life and make it more engaging for readers. Use strong verbs, descriptive adjectives, and sensory details to create vivid images in your reader's mind.

3. Be consistent: Consistency is key when it comes to narrative voice. Make sure that your voice is consistent throughout your story, from the dialogue to the narration.

4. Avoid cliches: Cliches can make your writing feel generic and unoriginal. Avoid using overused phrases and expressions, and strive to find fresh and unique ways of expressing yourself.

5. Edit and revise: Editing and revising are essential parts of the writing process. Take the time to review your work and make sure that your narrative voice is strong.

IV. Storytelling Strategies

- **How to structure an effective presentation: From opening to closing**

Effective storytelling is not limited to the world of fiction and non-fiction writing. It is also a crucial aspect of delivering an engaging and memorable presentation. Whether you are giving a business pitch, a TED Talk, or a lecture, having a clear and compelling narrative structure is key to capturing your audience's attention and conveying your message effectively.

In this chapter, we will explore the key elements of an effective presentation structure, from the opening to the closing. By following these guidelines, you can enhance your ability to deliver persuasive and engaging presentations that leave a lasting impression on your audience.

Opening

The opening of your presentation is the most critical part of the narrative structure, as it sets the tone for the entire presentation. It is your opportunity to capture the audience's attention and establish your credibility. There are several ways to create an effective opening:

1. Start with a compelling hook: This could be a surprising fact, a personal story, a powerful quote, or a rhetorical question. The goal is to pique the audience's curiosity and make them want to know more.

2. Use humor: Humor can be an excellent way to break the ice and connect with the audience on a personal level. However, be sure to use it judiciously and avoid offensive or inappropriate jokes.

3. State the purpose: Clearly articulate the purpose of your presentation, and what your audience will gain from listening to you. This helps set expectations and provides a roadmap for the rest of your presentation.

Body

The body of your presentation is where you develop your argument and support your key points. The body should be structured logically and clearly, with each point building upon the previous one. Here are some tips for structuring the body of your presentation:

1. Use a clear outline: Create a clear outline of your presentation that includes your main points, supporting evidence, and examples. This will help you stay focused and ensure that your argument flows logically.

2. Use stories and examples: Just as in writing, stories and examples are powerful tools for engaging your audience and making your points more memorable.

3. Use visuals: Visual aids such as charts, graphs, and images can help convey complex information quickly and effectively.

Closing

The closing of your presentation is your opportunity to leave a lasting impression on your audience and reinforce your key points. It should be clear, concise, and memorable. Here are some tips for creating an effective closing:

1. Summarize your key points: Summarize your main points in a clear and concise manner. This helps reinforce your argument and ensures that your audience leaves with a clear understanding of your message.

2. Use a call to action: If your presentation has a specific goal, such as persuading your audience to take a specific action, be sure to include a clear call to action.

3. End with a memorable statement: End your presentation with a memorable statement that encapsulates your message and leaves a lasting impression on your audience.

Delivery

Finally, delivery is just as important as the content of your presentation. Even the most well-structured presentation can fall flat if it is not delivered effectively. Here are some tips for delivering an effective presentation:

1. Practice, practice, practice: Practice your presentation until you feel confident and comfortable with the material. This will help reduce nervousness and ensure that you are able to deliver your message effectively.

2. Use body language: Use appropriate body language, such as hand gestures and facial expressions, to emphasize your points and convey enthusiasm and confidence.

3. Use vocal variety: Use vocal variety, such as changes in tone and pace, to keep your audience engaged and emphasize important points.

In conclusion, an effective presentation structure is crucial for delivering an engaging and memorable presentation. By following these guidelines, you can enhance your ability to connect with your audience, convey your message effectively and move to action.

- **How to use storytelling to persuade and sell: Techniques for storytelling in marketing and business**

Storytelling is a powerful tool in marketing and business, as it can capture the attention of potential customers and persuade them to take action. In fact, many successful businesses and brands have used storytelling to differentiate themselves from their competitors and create emotional connections with their target audience.

One of the key ways to use storytelling to persuade and sell is to understand the needs, desires, and pain points of your target audience. By understanding what your customers are looking for, you can create stories that resonate with them and show how your product or service can help them achieve their goals.

Another important aspect of using storytelling in marketing and business is to make sure your stories are authentic and genuine. Customers can tell when a story is contrived or insincere, and this can turn them off from your brand. Therefore, it is important to ensure that your stories reflect the values and beliefs of your brand, and that they are based on real experiences and examples.

There are several techniques that can be used to create effective storytelling in marketing and business. One popular technique is to use customer testimonials and case studies, which can demonstrate the effectiveness of your product or service in real-life situations. This can help build trust and credibility with your target audience, and make them more likely to consider your brand.

Another technique is to use storytelling to create a sense of urgency or scarcity around your product or service. By creating a narrative around the limited availability or high demand for your product, you can create a sense of excitement and anticipation among your target audience. This can make them more likely to take action and make a purchase before the opportunity passes them by.

Additionally, storytelling can be used to differentiate your brand from your competitors. By highlighting what makes your product or service unique, you can create a narrative that sets your brand apart from others in your industry. This can help you attract customers who are looking for something different or better than what is currently available.

When using storytelling in marketing and business, it is important to keep in mind that not all stories will be effective for every audience. Therefore, it is important to test and refine your storytelling techniques over time, and to be open to feedback from your target audience. By listening to their reactions and adjusting your approach accordingly, you can continue to improve the effectiveness of your storytelling and increase your chances of success.

In conclusion, storytelling can be a powerful tool for businesses and marketers looking to persuade and sell to their target audience. By understanding the needs and desires of your customers, creating authentic and genuine stories, and using effective techniques to differentiate your brand and create a sense of urgency, you can create a compelling narrative that captures the attention of potential customers and motivates them to take action. As with any marketing technique, it is important to continually test and refine your approach to ensure the best possible results.

- **How to use storytelling in leadership: How to inspire others and drive change through storytelling**

Leadership and storytelling are two seemingly unrelated concepts, but they are more intertwined than you might think. Great leaders know how to use the power of storytelling to inspire their followers, convey their vision, and drive change. Whether you are leading a team, a company, or an entire nation, the ability to tell compelling stories is a crucial skill that can make all the difference. In this chapter, we will explore how storytelling can be used in leadership and provide practical tips for using storytelling to inspire others and drive change.

Why Storytelling Matters in Leadership

Storytelling is a powerful tool for leaders because it enables them to connect with their followers on a deeper level. Stories have the ability to evoke emotions, spark imaginations, and create a shared sense of purpose. When leaders tell stories, they can inspire their followers to take action, to see things from a new perspective, and to feel a sense of belonging.

Moreover, storytelling is a more effective way to communicate complex ideas than facts and figures alone. By presenting ideas in the form of a story, leaders can make them more relatable, memorable, and understandable. When we hear a story, we are more likely to remember the details and to feel a personal connection to the message.

Examples of Storytelling in Leadership

There are countless examples of great leaders who have used storytelling to inspire their followers and drive change. Let's take a look at a few:

Martin Luther King Jr.: "I Have a Dream" speech

1. Perhaps one of the most famous examples of storytelling in leadership is Martin Luther King Jr.'s "I Have a Dream" speech. In this speech, King used vivid language and powerful imagery to convey his vision for a more just and equal society. By painting a picture of a future where all people are treated equally, King inspired millions of people to join the civil rights movement.

Steve Jobs: Apple product launches

2. Steve Jobs was a master storyteller who used Apple product launches as a platform for telling stories about the company's products. Jobs knew that people don't just buy products; they buy stories. By presenting

Apple's products as part of a larger narrative, Jobs was able to create a loyal following of customers who felt a personal connection to the brand.

Winston Churchill: wartime speeches

3.   During World War II, Winston Churchill used storytelling to rally the British people and inspire them to persevere in the face of adversity. Churchill's speeches were filled with vivid language, metaphors, and imagery that helped to create a sense of unity and purpose among the British people.

Tips for Using Storytelling in Leadership

Now that we have seen some examples of storytelling in leadership, let's explore some practical tips for using storytelling to inspire others and drive change:

Know your audience

1. To be an effective storyteller, you need to know your audience. What are their values, beliefs, and priorities? What are their hopes and fears? By understanding your audience, you can tailor your story to resonate with them on a deeper level.

Have a clear message

2.   Before you start telling your story, it's important to have a clear message in mind. What is the point you

are trying to make? What do you want your audience to take away from your story? Having a clear message will help you to stay focused and ensure that your story has a purpose.

Use vivid language and imagery

3.   To make your story more engaging and memorable, use vivid language and imagery. Paint a picture with your words and help your audience to see, hear, and feel what you are describing.

Be authentic

4.   Authenticity is key to effective storytelling. People can tell when you are not being genuine, and it will undermine your credibility. Be honest, vulnerable, and real, and your audience will respond

- **How to use storytelling for teaching and education: How to make information memorable through storytelling**

Storytelling has been a fundamental tool for teaching and education for centuries. From the oral tradition of passing down knowledge from generation to generation to modern-day classrooms, storytelling has always played a significant role in making information memorable and engaging for learners.

One of the main benefits of using storytelling in education is that it can help learners connect with the subject matter on a deeper level. By using narratives, educators can make complex or abstract concepts more relatable and understandable. Stories also help learners remember information more easily because they engage different parts of the brain than facts and figures alone.

So, how can educators effectively use storytelling to enhance their teaching and make information more memorable? Here are some tips:

1. Choose the right story: When selecting a story to share with learners, it's essential to consider the subject matter and the age group you are working with. The story should be appropriate for the audience and relevant to the lesson you are teaching.

2. Incorporate sensory details: To make a story more engaging, include sensory details that help learners visualize the setting, characters, and events. This technique helps to create a more immersive experience that learners can connect with on a deeper level.

3. Make the story interactive: To promote engagement and participation, consider making the story interactive. Ask learners to contribute to the story by adding details, predicting what might happen next, or even acting out parts of the story.

4. Use technology to enhance the story: With the increasing availability of technology, educators can use a range of tools to enhance their storytelling. This includes using multimedia, such

as images, videos, and sound effects, to create a more immersive and engaging experience.

5. Incorporate storytelling into lesson plans: Rather than seeing storytelling as a standalone activity, try to integrate it into your lesson plans. Use stories to introduce new concepts, reinforce learning, or provide context for a particular topic.

6. Encourage learners to create their own stories: Finally, encourage learners to create their own stories related to the subject matter. This technique promotes creativity and critical thinking while also helping learners to consolidate their understanding of the material.

In addition to these tips, there are several specific ways educators can use storytelling to enhance different aspects of teaching and education:

1. Teaching history and social studies: Storytelling can be an effective tool for teaching history and social studies. By using narratives, educators can bring historical events and figures to life, making them more relatable and engaging for learners. Stories can also help learners understand the social and cultural context of historical events and appreciate the perspectives of different groups.

2. Teaching language and literature: For language and literature classes, storytelling is a natural fit. Using stories can help learners improve their language skills by exposing them to new vocabulary, grammar structures, and idiomatic

expressions. Stories can also provide a window into different cultures and perspectives, promoting cross-cultural understanding.

3. Teaching science and math: While storytelling may seem less obvious for teaching science and math, it can still be a valuable tool. By using narratives, educators can provide context for scientific concepts and illustrate how they are relevant to real-world situations. Stories can also help learners develop problem-solving skills by presenting them with scenarios to analyze and resolve.

4. Promoting social-emotional learning: Storytelling can also be a powerful tool for promoting social-emotional learning. By sharing stories that illustrate empathy, resilience, and other important values, educators can help learners develop these skills and understand their importance.

In conclusion, storytelling is a powerful tool for enhancing teaching and education. By incorporating narratives into lessons and using techniques to make stories more engaging and memorable, educators can help learners connect with subject matter on a deeper level. Whether teaching history, language, science, or social-emotional skills, storytelling has the potential to make a significant impact on the learning experience.

V. The Future of Storytelling

- **The impact of artificial intelligence on storytelling: How technological tools are being used to enhance storytelling**

The impact of artificial intelligence on storytelling: How technological tools are being used to enhance storytelling

The art of storytelling has been around for thousands of years. From the earliest oral traditions to the written word and then film, it has evolved and adapted to new mediums and audiences. Now, in the age of technology, storytelling is once again transforming.

One of the biggest changes is the incorporation of artificial intelligence (AI) into the process. From the creation of characters to the production of content, AI is being used to enhance and improve storytelling in numerous ways.

One of the most significant ways in which AI is being used to enhance storytelling is through the creation of characters. Traditional character development involves the writer spending countless hours developing backstory, personality traits, and motivations. However, with the use of AI, these processes can be expedited and enhanced. AI can analyze vast amounts of data and information about a particular topic or demographic, allowing for the creation of more nuanced and authentic characters.

For example, in the creation of a historical figure or a character from a specific time period, AI can analyze countless books, articles, and primary sources to gain a better understanding of the person or era. This information can then be used to develop a more accurate and compelling character. Additionally, AI can analyze social media profiles and online activity to create characters that are more representative of modern society. This can lead to greater diversity and inclusion in storytelling, as AI can identify and incorporate perspectives and experiences that may have been overlooked in the past.

AI can also be used to improve the writing process itself. Many writers struggle with writer's block, finding it difficult to come up with new ideas or overcome creative barriers. However, with the use of AI, writers can receive prompts, suggestions, and even entire storylines that can help them overcome these obstacles. AI can analyze existing stories and identify patterns and themes, allowing writers to generate new ideas or improve upon existing ones.

Moreover, AI can help writers create more engaging and compelling stories by analyzing audience feedback and reactions. AI can analyze how readers or viewers respond to certain characters, plot points, and themes, providing valuable insights into what works and what doesn't. This can help writers refine their stories and tailor them to their target audience, resulting in more successful and impactful storytelling.

AI is also being used to improve the production process of storytelling. With the help of AI, filmmakers and animators can create more realistic and immersive environments and characters. AI can analyze real-life footage and photos to create digital backgrounds and settings that are more accurate and detailed than ever before. This can be particularly useful in historical or science-fiction storytelling, where accuracy and attention to detail are critical.

Additionally, AI can assist in the creation of special effects and animation. By analyzing real-life physics and movements, AI can create more realistic and believable effects, resulting in a more immersive and engaging experience for viewers. AI can also assist in the creation of digital actors and characters, allowing filmmakers and animators to create more lifelike and convincing performances.

However, while AI has the potential to greatly enhance and improve storytelling, it also raises concerns about the future of the industry. One of the most significant concerns is the potential for AI to replace human writers and storytellers. With the ability to analyze data and generate content, some fear that AI could eventually become the primary creators of stories, leaving human writers and artists behind.

Additionally, there are concerns about the ethical implications of AI-generated storytelling. With the ability to analyze vast amounts of data, there is a risk that AI could perpetuate biases and stereotypes that already exist in society. Furthermore, there are concerns about the potential for AI to manipulate or exploit audiences, particularly in the realm of advertising and marketing.

- **The future of media: How storytelling is adapting to technological and societal changes**

The world of media is constantly evolving, with new technologies and societal changes driving shifts in how stories are told and consumed. From the rise of streaming services to the increasing use of virtual and augmented reality, the future of media is exciting and full of possibilities. In this chapter, we will explore how storytelling is adapting to these changes and what the future of media may hold.

One of the most significant changes in recent years has been the rise of streaming services such as Netflix and Hulu. These platforms have disrupted traditional broadcast models, allowing for greater flexibility and choice in how and when viewers consume media. In response, traditional broadcasters have had to adapt, with many offering their own streaming services or partnering with existing platforms.

The rise of streaming services has also had an impact on storytelling. With entire seasons of shows available at once, binge-watching has become a popular way for viewers to consume media. This has led to changes in the way stories are told, with many shows now designed to be watched in a single sitting rather than over several weeks. This has also led to an increase in serialized storytelling, with shows designed to be watched in a particular order to fully appreciate the story.

However, the rise of streaming services has also raised concerns about the impact on traditional television and film industries. With viewers increasingly turning to streaming services, there are concerns that traditional broadcasters and cinemas may struggle to compete. Additionally, the financial models of streaming services have come under scrutiny, with some questioning whether the subscription-based model is sustainable in the long-term.

Another significant technological change that is impacting storytelling is the rise of virtual and augmented reality. These technologies offer new ways for audiences to experience stories, with the potential for greater immersion and interactivity. Virtual and augmented reality can transport viewers to different worlds, allowing them to explore and interact with the story in a more active and engaging way.

However, virtual and augmented reality also pose challenges for storytelling. Creating immersive and interactive experiences requires a different set of skills and approaches than traditional storytelling. Additionally, the high cost and technical requirements of virtual and augmented reality make it difficult for smaller creators and studios to compete.

Societal changes are also driving shifts in how stories are told and received. The rise of social media and the internet has given audiences greater power to shape the narrative and participate in the conversation. Audiences can now share their opinions and reactions to media in real-time, with creators and studios having to adapt to these changing expectations.

Additionally, there is a growing demand for diversity and representation in storytelling. Audiences are increasingly expecting to see themselves and their experiences reflected in media. This has led to a greater emphasis on diversity and inclusion in casting and storytelling, with creators and studios recognizing the importance of telling stories from different perspectives.

The growing awareness of social issues and activism is also driving changes in storytelling. Audiences are increasingly expecting media to engage with and comment on social and political issues, with creators and studios having to navigate these expectations. This has led to a rise in socially conscious storytelling, with creators using their platforms to raise awareness of important issues and effect change.

The future of media and storytelling is full of possibilities, but it also poses challenges and uncertainties. One of the biggest challenges is the potential for technological change to outpace the ability of creators and studios to adapt. With new technologies and platforms emerging at a rapid pace, it can be difficult for creators to keep up and deliver stories that take full advantage of these new possibilities.

Another challenge is the potential for media and storytelling to exacerbate societal issues and divisions. While media can be a powerful tool for raising awareness and effecting change, it can also perpetuate biases and stereotypes. Creators and studios need to keep in mind the potential impact of their stories and strive to create content that is truly positive and helps create a better world for all.

- **Final reflections on the power of storytelling and how it can help us create meaningful connections with others.**

Throughout this book, we have explored the power of storytelling and how it can be harnessed to unleash our narrative potential. We have seen how storytelling can be used to entertain, educate, persuade, and inspire, and how it can be a powerful tool for creating connections with others. In this final chapter, we will reflect on what we have learned and how we can continue to harness the power of storytelling in our lives.

At its core, storytelling is about making connections with others. Whether we are sharing a personal experience, conveying information, or trying to persuade someone, storytelling allows us to communicate in a way that resonates with others. When we tell stories, we invite others to enter our world and to see things from our perspective. This can create a sense of empathy and understanding, helping us to build stronger relationships with others.

One of the most powerful aspects of storytelling is its ability to evoke emotion. Stories can make us laugh, cry, and feel a wide range of emotions. When we hear a story that resonates with us, it can leave a lasting impression and influence how we think and feel. This emotional connection can help us to build stronger connections with others, as we share our feelings and experiences through the stories we tell.

However, storytelling is not just about the stories we tell. It is also about how we tell them. The way we communicate our stories can be just as important as the content itself. The tone, pacing, and delivery of a story can all influence how it is received and how it resonates with others. When we take the time to craft our stories carefully and thoughtfully, we can create a deeper connection with our audience.

Storytelling can also be a powerful tool for personal growth and development. When we tell stories about our own experiences, we are often forced to confront our own thoughts and feelings. This can help us to gain new insights and perspectives on ourselves and our lives. Additionally, when we share our stories with others, we invite them to provide feedback and support, which can help us to grow and develop in new ways.

Another important aspect of storytelling is its ability to inspire action. When we tell stories about social or political issues, we can motivate others to take action and effect change. By sharing stories about our own experiences with discrimination or injustice, we can inspire others to take up the fight for equality and justice. By sharing stories about the impact of climate change, we can inspire others to take steps to protect the environment.

In today's fast-paced, digital world, it can be easy to forget the power of storytelling. We are bombarded with information from all directions, and it can be difficult to cut through the noise and connect with others on a deeper level. However, the power of storytelling remains as strong as ever. Whether we are sharing stories with friends and family, creating content for social media, or delivering presentations at work, storytelling can be a powerful tool for creating meaningful connections with others.

As we look to the future, it is clear that storytelling will continue to play an important role in our lives. With new technologies and platforms emerging all the time, we have more opportunities than ever before to tell our stories and connect with others. However, it is important that we do not lose sight of the fundamentals of storytelling. Whether we are telling stories in person or online, we must remember that it is not just about the content of the story, but also about the way we communicate it and the connections we make with our audience.

In conclusion, storytelling is a powerful tool that can help us to connect with others on a deeper level. Whether we are sharing personal experiences, conveying information, or inspiring action, storytelling allows us to communicate in a way that resonates.

VI. Appendix

- **Practical exercises for crafting stories**
  1. Freewriting: Set a timer for 10 minutes and write without stopping. Let your thoughts flow and see where they take you. This can help you generate ideas and get your creative juices flowing.

  2. Character Development: Think of a character and write a detailed description of them. What do they look like? What are their likes and dislikes? What motivates them? This can help you create well-rounded and relatable characters.

  3. Dialogue Practice: Write a conversation between two characters. Focus on making the dialogue sound natural and engaging.

  4. Plotting: Create a plot outline for a story. Start with the beginning, middle, and end, and then fill in the details. This can help you organize your thoughts and create a clear structure for your story.

  5. Setting Description: Choose a location and write a detailed description of it. What does it look like? What does it smell like? What sounds can be heard there? This can help you create a vivid and immersive setting for your story.

6. Point of View: Write a scene from two different points of view. For example, write a scene from the perspective of two different characters or from a first-person and third-person perspective.

7. Conflict and Resolution: Write a scene where a character faces a conflict and must find a resolution. This can help you develop your storytelling skills by creating tension and resolution.

8. Theme Exploration: Choose a theme and write a story that explores it. For example, you could write a story about the importance of family or the consequences of greed.

9. Wordplay: Choose a word or phrase and write a story that incorporates it. This can help you develop your creative writing skills and expand your vocabulary.

10. Rewriting: Take a story you have written and rewrite it from a different perspective or with a different ending. This can help you see your story in a new light and make revisions to improve it.

These exercises can help you develop your storytelling skills and become a better writer. Remember to practice regularly and have fun with it!

- **Additional tips for storytelling**

1. Show, don't tell: Instead of simply telling your audience what's happening, show them through descriptive language and action. This can help create a more immersive and engaging experience for the reader.
2. Create memorable characters: Characters are often the heart of a story, so it's important to create ones that are well-rounded and memorable. Give them unique personalities, goals, and motivations that will keep the reader invested in their journey.

3. Use sensory details: Describing the sights, sounds, smells, tastes, and feelings in a scene can help bring it to life and create a more immersive experience for the reader.

4. Use foreshadowing: Foreshadowing can add an element of mystery and intrigue to your story. Hinting at future events or plot twists can keep the reader engaged and guessing.

5. Keep the plot moving: A story should have a clear beginning, middle, and end, but it's also important to keep the plot moving. Don't let the story get bogged down by unnecessary details or exposition.

6. Use conflict and tension: Conflict and tension are key elements of any story. Create obstacles for

your characters to overcome, and add tension by putting them in difficult or dangerous situations.

7. Use dialogue effectively: Dialogue can reveal character traits, advance the plot, and create tension. Make sure your dialogue is natural-sounding and serves a purpose in the story.

8. Be authentic: Write from your own experiences and emotions, and be true to your own voice. This can help create a sense of authenticity and honesty in your storytelling.

9. Edit and revise: Writing is a process, and it's important to revise and edit your work to make it the best it can be. Read through your story multiple times, and consider getting feedback from others.

10. Practice, practice, practice: The more you write, the better you will become at storytelling. Don't be afraid to experiment with different techniques and styles, and keep practicing until you find what works best for you.

- **Useful resources for writers and storytellers**

    1. Writing workshops and classes: Attending writing workshops and classes can provide valuable feedback and guidance from experienced writers and peers. Many universities and community centers offer writing workshops and classes.

    2. Writing organizations: Joining a writing organization such as the National Writers Association or the Science Fiction and

Fantasy Writers of America can provide networking opportunities, resources, and support for writers.

3. Writing conferences: Attending writing conferences can provide opportunities to meet other writers and industry professionals, attend workshops and panels, and pitch your work to agents and publishers.

4. Writing software and apps: Writing software and apps such as Scrivener, ProWritingAid, and Hemingway can help writers organize their work, improve their writing, and stay focused.

5. Online writing communities: Online writing communities such as Wattpad, Scribophile, and Critique Circle can provide feedback on your work, connect you with other writers, and offer writing prompts and challenges.

6. Writing blogs and websites: There are many writing blogs and websites that offer advice, resources, and inspiration for writers. Some popular ones include Writer's Digest, The Creative Penn, and Goins Writer.

7. Podcasts: Podcasts such as Writing Excuses and The Creative Penn offer advice and insights on writing and storytelling.

8. Books on writing: There are countless books on writing that can provide guidance and inspiration for writers. Some popular ones include On Writing by Stephen King, Bird by Bird by Anne Lamott, and The Elements of Style by William Strunk Jr. and E.B. White.

9. Writing contests: Entering writing contests can provide opportunities to get feedback on your work, gain exposure, and win prizes. Some popular writing contests include the Writer's Digest Annual Writing Competition and the BBC National Short Story Award.

10. Social media: Social media platforms such as Twitter, Instagram, and LinkedIn can provide opportunities to connect with other writers, agents, and publishers, and share your work with a wider audience.

As we come to the end of this journey through the power of storytelling, I want to take a moment to express my sincere gratitude to all those who have contributed to the creation of this book.

First and foremost, I want to thank the readers for investing their time and energy into exploring the art of storytelling. Your curiosity and dedication to learning is what motivates authors like myself to share our knowledge and experiences with the world.

I also want to express my appreciation to the countless storytellers, both past and present, who have inspired us with their incredible tales. From the ancient myths and legends to the modern works of literature, film, and television, your stories have shaped our understanding of the human experience and brought us together as a global community.

To my family and friends, thank you for your unwavering support and encouragement throughout this process. Your love and belief in me has been a constant source of strength and inspiration.

And finally, I want to acknowledge the power of storytelling itself. It is a force that has the ability to transcend time, space, and culture. It connects us to each other and to the world around us, giving us a deeper sense of meaning and purpose. I hope this book has provided you with the tools and insights you need to unleash your own narrative potential and tap into the transformative power of storytelling.

Thank you for joining me on this journey. May your stories continue to inspire, educate, and entertain for generations to come.

www.ingramcontent.com/pod-product-compliance
Lightning Source LLC
Chambersburg PA
CBHW071142220526
45467CB00015B/1746